LIBYA'S DESCENT

HEARING

BEFORE THE

COMMITTEE ON FOREIGN AFFAIRS
HOUSE OF REPRESENTATIVES

ONE HUNDRED THIRTEENTH CONGRESS

SECOND SESSION

SEPTEMBER 10, 2014

Serial No. 113–218

Printed for the use of the Committee on Foreign Affairs

Available via the World Wide Web: http://www.foreignaffairs.house.gov/ or
http://www.gpo.gov/fdsys/

U.S. GOVERNMENT PRINTING OFFICE

89–740PDF   WASHINGTON : 2014

For sale by the Superintendent of Documents, U.S. Government Printing Office
Internet: bookstore.gpo.gov   Phone: toll free (866) 512–1800; DC area (202) 512–1800
Fax: (202) 512–2104   Mail: Stop IDCC, Washington, DC 20402–0001

COMMITTEE ON FOREIGN AFFAIRS

EDWARD R. ROYCE, California, *Chairman*

CHRISTOPHER H. SMITH, New Jersey
ILEANA ROS-LEHTINEN, Florida
DANA ROHRABACHER, California
STEVE CHABOT, Ohio
JOE WILSON, South Carolina
MICHAEL T. McCAUL, Texas
TED POE, Texas
MATT SALMON, Arizona
TOM MARINO, Pennsylvania
JEFF DUNCAN, South Carolina
ADAM KINZINGER, Illinois
MO BROOKS, Alabama
TOM COTTON, Arkansas
PAUL COOK, California
GEORGE HOLDING, North Carolina
RANDY K. WEBER SR., Texas
SCOTT PERRY, Pennsylvania
STEVE STOCKMAN, Texas
RON DeSANTIS, Florida
DOUG COLLINS, Georgia
MARK MEADOWS, North Carolina
TED S. YOHO, Florida
SEAN DUFFY, Wisconsin
CURT CLAWSON, Florida

ELIOT L. ENGEL, New York
ENI F.H. FALEOMAVAEGA, American Samoa
BRAD SHERMAN, California
GREGORY W. MEEKS, New York
ALBIO SIRES, New Jersey
GERALD E. CONNOLLY, Virginia
THEODORE E. DEUTCH, Florida
BRIAN HIGGINS, New York
KAREN BASS, California
WILLIAM KEATING, Massachusetts
DAVID CICILLINE, Rhode Island
ALAN GRAYSON, Florida
JUAN VARGAS, California
BRADLEY S. SCHNEIDER, Illinois
JOSEPH P. KENNEDY III, Massachusetts
AMI BERA, California
ALAN S. LOWENTHAL, California
GRACE MENG, New York
LOIS FRANKEL, Florida
TULSI GABBARD, Hawaii
JOAQUIN CASTRO, Texas

AMY PORTER, *Chief of Staff*   THOMAS SHEEHY, *Staff Director*
JASON STEINBAUM, *Democratic Staff Director*

CONTENTS

LIBYA'S DESCENT

WEDNESDAY, SEPTEMBER 10, 2014

HOUSE OF REPRESENTATIVES,
COMMITTEE ON FOREIGN AFFAIRS,
Washington, DC.

The committee met, pursuant to notice, at 10:04 a.m., in room 2172 Rayburn House Office Building, Hon. Edward Royce (chairman of the committee) presiding.

Chairman ROYCE. We are going to ask if the members of the committee could take their seats and the witnesses as well. This hearing, entitled "Libya's Descent," will come to order. Less than 3 years ago Libya, at the time, if we think back, was hailed as a successful example of multilateral engagement—NATO and our allies all working together to stop the slaughter of civilians and to free an oppressed people from dictatorship, as was articulated at the time, to chart a prosperous path forward for this country in North Africa.

Unfortunately, in the ensuing years we have a situation since that date where the reality is that Libya has become chaotic, violent, awash in terrorist organizations and more militias than we can count. Its porous borders allow for the easy transit of people, of weapons, of money from conflicts across North Africa to Gaza to Syria to Iraq, and you have rival governments now in Tobruk and Tripoli making competing claims of legitimacy. Four months of fighting by the militias there—the last 4 months we have seen an additional ¼ million people flee Libya and "bring a climate of fear"—those are the words of the U.N. special report—"a climate of fear" across the country.

Given this downward spiral, it was not surprising that our Embassy in Tripoli had to be evacuated early this summer, and last week some of us saw the online videos of militants occupying that building. I think it reminded Americans of the deadly terrorist attack on our facility in Benghazi that took place 2 years ago when you see that occupation.

But you also saw these individuals doing belly flops into the pool. It was a reminder that you can't have a policy of neglect that then plays itself out into a humanitarian crisis and what, frankly, is a national security crisis.

So a U.N. Security Council has called for a cease fire and sanctions on those involved in the violence. But at the end of the day the rhetoric has not been matched up with leadership here and perhaps we should not be surprised that regional states conducted the air strikes on Libya last month.

(1)

Regional states are now attempting to affect their interests. They are hoping to help their favorite proxy in this conflict. Some suggest that Libya may even be headed for a partition or that neighboring Algeria or Egypt may intervene. We cannot allow Libya to become the Lebanon of the 1970s and 1980s. We remember what happened in Lebanon. We remember how long society struggled with the aftermath of that situation, and what happened in Lebanon was that regional states played out their feuds at the expense of the local population. And if that is to be avoided, then Libya needs immediate attention. As we will hear today, the administration is pushing all sides toward a political solution.

But I don't see this happening without real pressure on the factions, real leverage on those factions. Others advocate for cutting off outside support for militias and compelling their disarmament through threat of force. Such action would have to be coupled with programs to unlock Libya's wealth in order to train a security force for all Libyans.

But given how poorly the U.S. and coalition partners have worked on Libya to date, it is tough to see such an effort coming together. We have not really had a desire to lead in Libya and it is an absolutely necessity, I think, right now, that the administration lay out a strategy to lead in Libya.

We need to hear testimony today on the administration's plan to respond to the very real threats to national security that a failed Libya represents, and we need to also hear about the different proposals for action in Libya that are being discussed at the United Nations, at NATO, and among other North African countries.

We need to hear what those options are, what those discussions are. Libya and every conflict is, of course, rooted in local conditions but the many Middle Eastern conflicts do share a driving force of extremism, jihadists fueled by radical ideology, armed and funded from outside the immediate area.

In this case, again, not surprisingly, Qatar is up to its elbows in funding terrorist activity there or funding some of these militias but other countries as well have their proxies.

It is a deadly accelerant that the administration has been slow in recognizing and countering and part of this hearing today is to bring some focus on it and bring some strategy into it.

So I would now like to turn to our ranking member, Mr. Ted Deutch of Florida, for his opening remarks. I would mention that Eliot Engel was in New York for Primary Day yesterday so he is on his way back and so ranking today is Mr. Ted Deutch.

Mr. DEUTCH. Thank you, Mr. Chairman. What began in Libya as the successful overthrow of the dictator Muammar Gaddafi has tragically devolved into an environment that appears to have put the country on the brink of becoming a failed state.

There were plans in place after the revolution in 2011 that offered promising signs such as the formation of national institutions, the reintegration of militias into a new national military force.

But the Libya we see today is not the Libya that the Libyan people who suffered so long under Gaddafi nor the world envisioned. In late June of this year, the Subcommittee on the Middle East and

North Africa held a hearing on Libya, entitled ''Libya at a Cross-roads.''

Now, just months later it appears that Libya is on a path away from democracy and stability and toward increased violence and fragmentation. The fracturing of Libya's elected and state institutions has left the country incapable of producing or implementing any effective policies.

The recently elected House of Representatives has fled to the eastern city of Tubruk while the unrecognized reformed General National Congress dominated by Islamist former MPs sits in the capitol of Tripoli.

The National Security Force had never achieved sole control over security within its borders and has now suffered from defections and divisions. Most of the country is now dominated by various militant groups vying for control, weaving an inconsistent patchwork of loyalties throughout the country.

The security situation has deteriorated to the point that Libya's airport and much of Tripoli are dominated by Islamist militias. The U.S. Government has relocated our Embassy staff amid reports that a force aligned with a Libya Dawn coalition is now claiming to be guarding our abandoned Embassy. Fear that unrest inside Libya will not be contained within its borders is permeating the region.

The instability has created an environment where transnational extremist groups can easily travel in and out of the country and porous borders have allowed for the easy flow of weapons and foreign fighters.

Following their respective revolutions, Egypt to Libya's east and Tunisia to the northwest have worked hard to resist the pressures of radical militant groups from causing significant unrest and moving their countries backward.

But having a failed state as a neighbor, in which terrorist groups are free to consolidate and grow and are given free access to significant amounts of weapons and resources, is not a reality that either country can accept. So the question now remains: Who on the ground can be a partner for the international community?

There is no neat division of loyalty among the Libyan people and it is difficult to determine which parties share our interests. The members of the House of Representatives were elected only a few months ago, albeit with a very low voter turnout.

Possibly for this reason it lacks recognition and legitimacy for many Libyans. The alternative body, the GNC, defied the political roadmap in the Libyan constitution by creating a parallel government separate from the elected body.

General Haftar's forces have been fighting Islamist groups including Ansar al-Sharia, the group responsible for the attack on our Benghazi mission nearly 2 years ago that led to the tragic death of Ambassador Chris Stevens and three other Americans. But his forces have faced recent setbacks and his political intentions are not entirely clear.

It also remains unclear what role other countries in the region are playing in Libya's internal affairs. Nevertheless, I believe the United States must remain engaged in Libya.

We must encourage a political process that results in the recognition of one legitimate government and continue to offer support through good governance, democracy assistance, and rule of law development programs.

We must remain ready to assist in the training of a Libyan General Purpose Force that is capable of reclaiming security control in the country and encourage the Libyan Government to take steps to finally commence this program.

As I have said, Libya's neighbors have a vested interest in restoring stability to Libya. The United Nations has committed a point person to work on negotiating a cease fire between the various factions.

But the international community must be clear that continued support for extremist Islamist groups by regional actors cannot be tolerated.

Libya has a long way to go to repair the 42 years of Gaddafi's rule, in which he tore down any semblance of democratic governance and functioning institutions and ultimately the future of Libya is in the hands of the Libyan people.

Ambassador Feierstein, I look forward to your testimony to hear how the State Department is determining the best approach for the United States to take to prevent Libya from indeed becoming a failed state, and I yield back.

Chairman ROYCE. Thank you, Mr. Deutch. We go to the chair of the Subcommittee on the Middle East and North Africa, Ms. Ileana Ros-Lehtinen of Florida, for 1 minute.

Ms. ROS-LEHTINEN. Thank you so much, Mr. Chairman, for holding this timely hearing. As Mr. Deutch pointed out, our Subcommittee on the Middle East and North Africa held a hearing with State Department officials on Libya's faltering transition months ago and here we are again, only Libya's deteriorating situation has gotten worse and Libya is teetering on the brink of becoming a failed state.

After the air campaign in Libya in 2011, the Obama administration turned its back on the long-term engagement that Libya desperately needed for a smoother transition.

The political narrative that all was swell in Libya created a breeding ground for the terrorist attack against Americans in our consulate in Benghazi. After this void it was replaced by militias, terrorist organizations, and other nonstate actors that are ripping this country apart.

We want a concrete plan from the administration to address how it is working to prevent Libya from turning into a larger safe haven for terrorists and posing a serious threat to the region and U.S. national security.

Thank you, Mr. Chairman.

Chairman ROYCE. Thank you, Chairwoman. We are going to go to—for 1 minute to Gerry Connolly of Virginia with the Middle East Subcommittee and then to the chairman of the Subcommittee on Terrorism, Nonproliferation, and Trade, Judge Ted Poe of Texas, for a minute.

Mr. CONNOLLY. Thank you, Mr. Chairman, and welcome, Mr. Ambassador.

I very much respect my dear friend, Ms. Ros-Lehtinen of Florida, but I cannot accept the gratuitous potshot at the administration as if this President and the administration are responsible for what has transpired in Libya.

Many of the same current critics criticized the administration for not being more active in Libya at the time of the revolution.

There are internal forces in Libya that have to be understood and that are far beyond American control and the reign of militias is one of them. When I went to visit Libya, security at the airport was provided by a militia. That was over 2 years ago, and unfortunately the situation seems to have deteriorated.

So I think it is really important, and this I do agree with Ms. Ros-Lehtinen—we can't look at the Libya situation with rose-colored glasses. We have got to figure out what are our next steps forward and what, if anything, can be done to try to put us on a path toward stable governance. Thank you, Mr. Chairman.

Chairman ROYCE. Thank you. Mr. Poe.

Mr. POE. No question about it, Gaddafi was a bad guy. But when the United States decided to remove his legitimate government and overthrow him, that was, to me, a strategic political mistake that has consequences we see today.

Now, such decision, of course, was made without congressional approval. When the United States gave the green light to Qatar to send weapons to Libya and spread the conflict, it spread throughout North Africa including to the terrorist group AQIM.

AQIM used those weapons to take over a gas plant in Algeria and kill one of my constituents, Victor Lovelady, and two other Americans. Of course, we know about the U.S. Ambassador and three other Americans killed in Benghazi.

When Gaddafi was gone, radicals of different stripes including some affiliated with al-Qaeda had filled the vacuum. The Government of Libya cannot govern because it has no functional army and to me it is a failed state.

The people support the militia groups because they are the ones—they provide the security so people support them. Now the United States has pulled out of Libya, leaving terrorists to play in the swimming pools owned by the United States.

Libya today is a result of a policy of removing a government without congressional approval because we don't like them. We are not safer because Gaddafi is gone. The world is not safer and Libya is in chaos, and I yield back.

Chairman ROYCE. This morning we are pleased to be joined by Ambassador Gerald Feierstein, Principal Deputy Assistant Secretary for the Bureau of Near Eastern Affairs.

Prior to his current position, he was the United States Ambassador to Yemen from 2010 to 2013—tough post—and he joined the Foreign Service in June of '75 and has served overseas in eight different postings including Islamabad, Tunis, Riyadh and Beirut—tougher posts.

The Ambassador also served as principal deputy assistant coordinator and deputy assistant coordinator for programs in the Bureau of Counterterrorism from '06 to '08.

Without objection, we are going to have the witness' full prepared statement be made part of the record and members here will have 5 calendar days in which they can submit any statements or questions or any extraneous material for the record.

So Ambassador Feierstein, if you would please summarize your remarks. We will go 5 minutes and then ask you questions. Thank you.

STATEMENT OF THE HONORABLE GERALD FEIERSTEIN, PRINCIPAL DEPUTY ASSISTANT SECRETARY, BUREAU OF NEAR EASTERN AFFAIRS, U.S. DEPARTMENT OF STATE

Mr. FEIERSTEIN. Thank you very—thank you very much, Chairman Royce, Ranking Member Deutch, members of the committee, for giving me this opportunity to come here today and to discuss the situation in Libya and the administration's response.

Since the 2011 revolution, millions of Libyans have expressed high hopes that the country will seize the opportunity provided by the overthrow of the Gaddafi regime to build a new state based on strong democratic institutions and providing a secure, stable framework that would put Libya's vast energy resources to work on behalf of the Libyan people.

Instead, Libya's new political institutions and leaders have failed to beat Libya's challenges. Despite the efforts of many brave Libyans as well as the active engagement of the United States and our international partners, too many of Libya's power brokers and militia commanders have rejected principles of dialogue, consensus building, and compromise in favor of pursuit of narrow-minded interests and a scramble for control of Libya's resources.

The weak central government ravaged by 42 years of Gaddafi's misrule has proven incapable of providing security, governance or access to economic opportunity. In the absence of capable government, opportunistic criminals, militias, and terrorist groups are battling for control.

Internecine clashes have been fuelled by domestic weapons stockpiles and flows of fighters and weapons as a result of the government's inability to secure Libya's long porous borders.

In recent months, hundreds of Libyan civilians have died as a result of the conflict and the United Nations reports that ¼ million people inside Libya have been displaced since the recent clashes began.

Critical Libyan public infrastructure including Libya's major airports in Benghazi and in Tripoli have also been targeted by rival militias. Indeed, the conflict in parts of the country is best understood primarily as a struggle over resources and power and only secondarily over ideology.

Clearly, Libya cannot move forward without addressing its lawlessness and violence and it cannot address the violence without achieving a basic political framework for the path forward.

But Libya's political transition has stalled and in recent weeks the government itself has fractured into two competing groups based in different cities, Tripoli and Tubruk, even as most of the international community has been forced by the violence to leave the country.

As fighting escalated in the Tripoli neighborhood where our Embassy is located, the United States decided to suspend operations temporarily and withdraw U.S. personnel from the country. Ambassador Jones and a small team have relocated to our Embassy in Malta from which they continue to carry out their diplomatic and assistance duties.

It remains in United States interests to help remove Libya from this cycle of violence. We want to see the fighting end and competing factions commit to settling their differences through a process of dialogue and negotiation.

In fact, despite the violence, we do see a potential path forward. There are still many in Libya who understand that their country needs an inclusive government that shares power and resources in a fair and transparent way.

We are working closely with the United Nations, the European Union, and other European partners to advance a unified approach, encouraging all Libyans to adopt basic principles of nonviolence and commit to a democratic state.

We are working to promote these principles directly with Libyans from across the country and the political spectrum. We and our allies also have a number of coordinated assistance programs designed to help Libyans build a secure, democratic and prosperous state that continues to operate through local staff and existing networks on the ground.

Libyan spoilers need to understand that there are consequences for violence and for actions that threaten Libya's democratic transition. Consistent with that, we were able to work with the members of the U.N. Security Council 2 weeks ago to secure unanimous approval of a new resolution, U.N. SCR 2174, that provides for targeted U.N. sanctions against those who undermine the political transition process.

We also are reaching out to Libya's neighbors and to others in the region and beyond who have a strong interest in seeing a stable, secure and democratic Libya. Our goal is to seek these countries' support in pushing all Libyan factions into a productive political process. Envisioning a peaceful and prosperous Libya can be challenging, particularly when the trajectory is negative. But if Libya could overcome its discord, it has unique advantages that could support the advancement of the democratic transition process and facilitate building the state. If Libya's political factions were to work together instead of fighting, they could boost oil and other exports to capacity and use the proceeds to invest in Libya's infrastructure, its health and education systems and, most importantly, its people.

With a population of only 6 million, Libya offers enormous opportunities. Supporting a political resolution to the current impasse so that we can advance Libyans' efforts to build a democratic state remains one of the United States' top foreign policy goals.

Thank you, Mr. Chairman, and I stand to answer questions from the committee.

[The prepared statement of Mr. Feierstein follows:]

Statement for the Record
Ambassador Gerald Feierstein
Principal Deputy Assistant Secretary of State for Near Eastern Affairs

House Foreign Affairs Committee
September 10, 2014

Thank you, Chairman Royce, Ranking Member Engel, and Members of the Committee for inviting me to discuss the situation in Libya today and the Administration's response.

Since the 2011 revolution, millions of Libyans have expressed high hopes that the country will seize the opportunity provided by the overthrow of the Qadhafi regime to build a new state, based on strong democratic institutions and providing a secure, stable framework that would put Libya's vast energy resources to work on behalf of the Libyan people.

Instead, Libya's new political institutions and leaders have failed to meet Libya's challenges. Despite the efforts of many brave Libyans as well as the active engagement of the United States and our international partners, too many of Libya's power brokers and militia commanders have rejected principles of dialogue, consensus building, and compromise in favor of pursuit of narrow-minded interests and a scramble for control of Libya's resources. The weak central government, ravaged by 42 years of Qadhafi's misrule, has proven incapable of providing security, governance, or access to economic opportunity.

In the absence of capable government, opportunistic criminals, militias, and terrorist groups are battling for control. Internecine clashes have been fueled by domestic weapons stockpiles and flows of fighters and weapons as a result of the government's inability to secure Libya's long, porous borders. In recent months, hundreds of Libyan civilians have died as a result of the conflict, and the UN reports that a quarter million people inside Libya have been displaced or fled since recent clashes began. Critical Libyan public infrastructure, including Libya's major airports in Tripoli and Benghazi, has also been targeted by rival militias. Indeed, the conflict in parts of the country is best understood primarily as a struggle over resources and power, and only secondarily over ideology.

Clearly, Libya cannot move forward without addressing its lawlessness and violence, and it cannot address the violence without achieving a basic political framework for the path forward. But Libya's political transition has stalled, and in recent weeks the government itself has fractured into two competing groups based in different cities – Tripoli and Tobruk – even as most of the international community has been forced by the violence to leave the country. As fighting escalated in the Tripoli neighborhood where our embassy is located, the United States decided to suspend operations temporarily and withdraw U.S personnel from the country. Ambassador Jones and a small team have relocated to our embassy in Malta, from where they continue to carry out their diplomatic and assistance duties.

It remains in the United States' interest to help remove Libya from this cycle of violence. We want to see the fighting end and competing factions commit to settling their differences through a process of dialogue and negotiation. In fact, despite the violence, we do see a potential path forward. There are still many in Libya who understand their country needs an inclusive government that shares power and resources in a fair and transparent way. We are working closely with the United Nations, the European Union, and with other European partners to advance a unified approach, encouraging all Libyans to adopt basic principles of non-violence and commit to a democratic state. We are working to promote these principles directly with Libyans from across the country and the political spectrum. We and our allies also have a number of coordinated assistance programs designed to help Libyans build a secure, democratic, and prosperous state that continue to opearate through local staff and existing networks on the ground .

Libyan spoilers need to understand that there are consequences for violence and for actions that threaten Libya's democratic transition. Consistent with that, we were able to work with the members of the UN Security Council two weeks ago to secure unanimous approval of a new resolution, UNSCR 2174, that provides for targeted UN sanctions against those who undermine the political transition process.

We also are reaching out to Libya's neighbors and to others in the region and beyond who have a strong interest in seeing a stable, secure, and democratic Libya. Our goal is to seek these countries' support in pushing all Libyan factions into a productive political process. Positive engagement by regional actors can help Libya. The Tunis Process, a neighbors group made up of Algeria, Tunisia, Egypt, Chad, Niger and Sudan, meets regularly to coordinate engagement with Libya. In August, the group met in Cairo for its fourth ministerial and called for non-interference in Libya's internal affairs and support for a political process to resolve the Libyan conflict. These developments are encouraging.

It is vital that we continue to pursue this avenue. Libya's location means that its challenges pose a grave threat to the overall security of the Sahel, North Africa, and the greater Mediterranean. Terrorist groups continue to take advantage of the lawlessness to build their capabilities and neither the U.S. nor Libya's friends and neighbors will accept any attempt to use Libya as a base to launch attacks against our interests in the region and the world. Accordingly, while opposing outside intervention in Libya by any foreign power, we continue to seek ways to counter those who seek to use Libya or Libyans in the cause of terrorism.

Envisioning a peaceful and prosperous Libya can be challenging, particularly when the trajectory is negative. But if Libya could overcome its discord, it has unique advantages that could support the advancement of the democratic transition process and facilitate building the state. If Libya's political factions were to work together instead of fighting, they could boost oil and other exports to capacity and use the proceeds to invest in Libya's infrastructure, its health and education systems, and most importantly, its people. With a population of only six million, Libya offers enormous opportunities. Supporting a political resolution to the current impasse, so that we can advance Libyans' efforts to build a democratic state, remains one of the United States' top foreign policy goals.

Thank you, Mr. Chairman. I would be pleased to answer questions from the Committee.

———————

Chairman ROYCE. Ambassador, thank you. Thank you very much. A couple of quick questions.

One has been, how to pronounces this—Khoms, the town 125 miles east of Tripoli that we read about where it is sort of the favorite jumping off point for these fighters that are headed to ISIL. Can——

Mr. FEIERSTEIN. There is Derna.

Chairman ROYCE. Well, the region—let us just talk about the region in general in the east. That is where so many of these key al-Qaeda fighters came from in the past and now we see these ISIS fighters coming out of that area.

Can you provide any more detail there about the route that they are taking, you know, to get into the Iraq-Syria fight? And then last week, we saw the story about the plane from Sudan landing near the Libyan-Sudanese border and the government in Libya claims that the plane was full of weapons, destined for the Islamist Libya Dawn and for that militia, and in response you saw the Sudanese military attache being expelled.

The Sudanese Government denied it, but at the same time you had a situation where President Bashir warmly received the Islamist party representative, the President of the former Libyan General National Congress in Khartoum last week.

So we see that internecine situation where they are engaged. You see that Qatar, which is not only engaged here but with al-Nusra—funding al-Nusra, and then 90 percent of Hamas—they tell us that 90 percent of Hamas' funding is now coming from Qatar.

What can you tell us about these outside countries' interests and who they are funding here and also the connection to these young fighters getting whipped up and ending up enlisting with ISIL?

Mr. FEIERSTEIN. Thank you, Mr. Chairman, and all of those are important questions.

In terms of the flow of foreign fighters, I don't think that there is one single route that they—that they pursue to get to Syria or to Iraq. There are a number of different ways that they transit from Libya into Europe, into Turkey, directly into Syria.

So one of the things, of course, that we are talking about in terms of what we are going to try to accomplish in confronting ISIL and, as the President said, in defeating ISIL, is, in fact, to work with our friends and partners around the world to cut off this flow of foreign fighters and there are a number of different steps that we need to take to do that and the State Department—Ambassador Bradtke—is very much involved in visiting and particularly in North Africa where we do have serious concerns about the movement of foreign fighters.

Chairman ROYCE. Yes, but what is happening is that Sudan and other countries are playing this role in creating absolute chaos and out of chaos is coming, you know, more enlistments.

What role is Sudan playing right now in Libya? In the past, we have talked about the role Sudan played, you know, in supporting groups like the Lord's Resistance Army—Joseph Kony—in trying to destabilize the Democratic Republic of Congo and Uganda and Central African Republic.

Well, you know, here is Sudan again playing a role. What can you tell us about that role?

Mr. FEIERSTEIN. Yes, sir, and certainly the reports that you mentioned of flights from Sudan bringing weapons into Libya—we are very aware of those.

It is a serious problem. We have taken a broad position not only with the Qataris and the Sudanese but across the board that foreign intervention inside of Libya is unhelpful, it is deepening divisions within that society.

It is provocative. It is promoting the very conflict that we believe is the major obstacle and so we are looking—there is a process under way—it is called the Tunis process—that brings together Libya's neighbors in ways that we think are constructive and helpful, and they met 2 weeks ago in Cairo and issued a very helpful statement which basically said that they are opposed to foreign involvement, foreign intervention in Libyan affairs. Sudan is part of that process and we will be looking to them for—to stop.

Chairman ROYCE. Well, I understand. Ambassador, I wish your testimony made me feel better about the direction we are headed.

I think that the reality is whatever our protestations and whatever people are signing in terms of these statements of disapproval, the reality is that Qatar and Sudan and other states are pouring in weapons, pouring in money and creating the instability, the chaos, out of which comes the threat, and I think we need a strategy for what we are going to do—not say—but what we are going to do with respect to the emir of Qatar.

We need a strategy in terms of what we are going to do with Khartoum. But anyway, my time has expired. I will go to Mr. Ted Deutch.

Mr. DEUTCH. Thank you, Mr. Chairman. Ambassador Feierstein, understanding that this might be classified, can you comment on the reported action taken by the Egyptians and the Emiratis in Libya and what are the ramifications of this kind of foreign action at this point, given the internal chaos within the country?

Mr. FEIERSTEIN. Thank you, Mr. Deutch, and as you suggested, it is difficult to talk about that issue in this setting. But we would be happy to come back and speak to you in a classified setting and provide you with a fuller brief on what we know about those issues.

But I would say that, as a general principle whenever there are allegations like this, we do investigate them and we will try to make sure that we understand what happened.

But, again, it goes back to the general principle, which is what we see as the—as the danger of this foreign engagement and the fact is that as long as we have this conflict going on inside of Libya it is going to invite unhelpful engagement by outside parties who are going to use this as an opportunity to pursue their own goals, their own agendas.

And so the strategy that we have is to try to bring the Libyans together, end the conflict inside of Libya and the violence and begin a political process that will close off the opportunities that outside actors have to engage unhelpfully inside of Libya.

Mr. DEUTCH. All right. Thank you. I hope we have the opportunity to pursue that further in the appropriate setting. The prospect of Libya as a terrorist safe haven isn't just a U.S. problem. It is a problem for the international community, particularly our European friends, given the proximity.

What is our assessment of the links between the militants in Libya and other al-Qaeda-affiliated groups and do we know at this point whether Libyan fighters are joining ISIL's ranks?

Mr. FEIERSTEIN. The links, of course, we do have—as was mentioned in the opening statements, we do have a longstanding issue with al-Qaeda and the Islamic Maghreb—AQIM—which has been a concern for many years. We watch very closely.

There have been some who have expressed interest in joining their programs, their organizations with ISIL. We haven't actually seen that happen yet.

We are certainly concerned about Libyan fighters who are going to Syria or Iraq to join the fight there. It goes back to the concern that we have overall about the flow of foreign fighters and the need to stop that.

So all of these remain concerns and issues that are high in our agenda. In terms of what we are doing, absolutely correct that the Europeans are extremely concerned about this.

We have the European Union's border assistance organization, EUBAM, that has established and has been trying to push a program inside of Libya that would help secure Libyan borders.

In terms of our own activities, we are supporting EUBAM but we are also working with Libya's neighbors—with the Egyptians, with Tunisia, with Algeria—to try to help them strengthen their border security.

We are also, of course, very concerned about the flow of weapons and trying to remove weapons from Libya and prevent the flow of new weapons, and the U.N. Security Resolution 2174 includes new language on preventing the flow of weapons inside of Libya.

So we are working across a number of different avenues of effort to try to prevent the flow of fighters and weapons in and out of Libya and to provide greater security.

Mr. DEUTCH. Thank you. I am—I hope over the course of this hearing you will have an opportunity to speak to the broader issue of the reason that we should continue to be involved in Libya.

Hopefully, you will have a chance to speak to the State Department's view of not just why Libya is important—you have spoken about that some, we have all spoken about that—but what is—where are we going.

All of our discussions, understandably, are focused on the near term and the intermediate term. Long term, though, what do you expect Syria to—Libya, rather, to look like in 5 years? In 10 years?

What is the best that we can actually hope for? And I am out of time but I do hope that you will have a chance to speak to that. I yield back.

Ms. ROS-LEHTINEN. Thank you so much, Mr. Deutch. Welcome, Mr. Ambassador.

As Mr. Deutch pointed out, our subcommittee held a hearing months ago on Libya, the same day that elections were being held in that country, and while there may have been a cautious optimism that the June 25 elections could have been an important step toward stability in Libya, during the hearing I made it clear that the timing of the elections was rushed because it was announced only 1 month before the elections were going to take place.

So it is not surprising that the elections ultimately failed to bring about a large turnout nor the much desired path toward democracy and the rule of law in Libya, and during that hearing Ambassador Patterson was optimistic that the elections in Libya, which were the third in less than 2 years, would be an important step forward toward Libya's stability.

Now we see that that was misplaced optimism as the situation is worse than ever. I cautioned then that as long as the security situation remained tenuous in Libya so too will the political will and the transition stall and that Libya's economy would continue to falter.

So given the fact that your testimony admits that there is an absence of a capable government, why were elections rushed at the time when we knew that it wasn't sustainable for the long term?

And I agree that elections are important but it is just one part of a democracy and only when there is a political will to govern effectively and inclusively.

The fighting in Libya continues to be overshadowed by a struggle between secular forces against Islamists, but with over 1,600 militias in this country this characterization is actually oversimplified, but just in terms of trying to grab the enormity of the problem— 1,600 militias.

In our subhearing, Assistant Secretary Patterson said, ''The most urgent objective we have is for counterterrorism.'' Yet, 3 years after Gaddafi and over a year after the U.S. committed to train the General Purpose Force, GPF, not a single one of the 5,000 to 8,000 planned forces has in fact been trained.

Seeing the need now more than ever for a security force in Libya, why has this project not gotten off the ground?

How else do we plan on combating the terrorist threat that is growing within Libya, short of direct U.S. intervention? And not only has the internal fighting deteriorated but it has already become a regional conflict. Unsecure borders allow extremists and weapons smugglers unhindered access into the country.

And then my third question is about the Friends of Libya Summit. I know that these entities have been meeting off and on. It was announced earlier that the U.N. General Assembly, the African Union, and the Spanish Government will hold this Friends of Libya Summit in Madrid.

Is this going to happen or is it just a continuation of what has— the meetings that have already taken place? Is Egypt trying to get support for its 10-point plan on Libya? Because I notice that in your testimony you don't highlight that. Does the State Department endorse this plan or not?

So my questions are the three questions: The General Purpose Force training, what is the status of that?; looking back, do we feel that we were rushing the election process and being too enthusiastic about it?; and the Friends of Libya Summit, Egypt's 10-point plan—are we endorsing that and what is happening?

Thank you, sir.

Mr. FEIERSTEIN. Thank you, Ms. Ros-Lehtinen. In terms of the three specific points, the General Purpose Force is still something that we want to pursue.

It is something that we have discussed with Prime Minister al-Thani and the other senior leadership. We had an opportunity to talk about that when he was here for the Africa Summit a couple of weeks ago.

They, subsequently to those meetings, actually signed the letter of agreement for the GPF and, of course, a part of the issue there is the funding for it and their obligation to pay for the training. But we are working on that and we hope to move forward.

So as soon as circumstances permit, it is still our commitment and our—and our desire to move forward on the General Purpose Force. We continue to see that as an important element of the overall security framework for Libya, going forward.

Ms. ROS-LEHTINEN. Thank you, sir. I asked too many questions and I blab on too much. So I hope that you get to the answers through another venue. Thank you so much.

Mr. FEIERSTEIN. Thank you, ma'am.

Ms. ROS-LEHTINEN. Dr. Bera of California is recognized.

Mr. BERA. Thank you, Chairwoman. Libya continues to show the difficult transition from autocratic authoritarian regimes to democracy or some form of democracy.

I mean, we have seen it—seen the difficulty in Iraq and we have seen the turmoil for decades in Lebanon and, again, Libya proves that it is not a straight shot.

You know, I think playing off of the question that my colleague from Florida, Mr. Deutch, asked, what does the long term look like in Libya as well as some of these other states that are making this transition?

Mr. FEIERSTEIN. Thank you for the question, and I think that as I alluded in my opening statement, our view is that Libya is still a country with enormous potential. It has, of course, as we know, huge energy resources and established infrastructure that can—that can export those resources primarily to Europe, which is their major customer.

It is a relatively small population. We believe that with the proper investment in health and education it is a population that will be able to manage Libyan affairs very successfully.

We believe and are committed to trying to help Libya develop the governmental institutions that would allow it to build a stable democratic society and we also believe that this is what the majority of Libyans desire.

So I think that our view is that the path forward, if we can stabilize the situation now; end the violence, get a political process moving that allows Libyans to come to a negotiating table and work out their differences, if we can do those things then the international community including the United States, including Libya's neighbors and the countries of Europe are standing by to support the development of the institutions that will allow them to move forward successfully into the future.

Mr. BERA. So you touched on a key point. So if we look at our own democracy here in America, time and time again we have demonstrated when threatened we are willing to step up and fight and die to protect our freedom and democracy.

You mentioned that, Ambassador, that the Libyan people desire that democracy or that stability. Do you have a sense that they are willing to step up and fight against, you know, the militias that, you know, potentially are tearing their country apart?

I mean, again, democracy, for it to have long-term stability, has to come from within and the people have to be willing to fight for it.

Mr. FEIERSTEIN. We couldn't agree more and I think that the Libyan people demonstrated during the resistance in 2011 to Muammar Gaddafi and the clique around him that they are prepared to stand up and to fight and to die in defense of their values and I do think, again, that what we see is still the critical mass of Libyans who are ready to do that, who are ready to work with us, the international community, ready to work with each other to try to build the kind of society that they would like to see for the future.

Mr. BERA. Great, and I have got two last questions. I will try to get them in here. What percentage of the destabilizing forces in these militias are actually coming external from Libya, that are not fighting for the interests of the Libyan people?

Mr. FEIERSTEIN. To the best of our knowledge and understanding, sir, we believe that there are not very many foreign fighters inside of Libya. This is mostly militias who were drawn from the Libyan population.

Mr. BERA. Okay. And lastly, if we look at the Arab Spring in total, it is interesting. The one country where the Arab Spring purportedly started—Tunisia—while not without its own challenges, appears to be relatively stable in this. Are there any contrasts that we can draw or lessons that we can learn from Tunisia?

Mr. FEIERSTEIN. Tunisia is, of course, in our view, as you said, one of the states that has most successfully moved into this political transition period.

I think that you could say that Tunisia, over the course of its independent history, had a number of governmental institutions that continue to function and that continue to provide a framework for this successful transition.

I think also we should credit the wisdom of the Tunisian political leadership, the people who actually came to power after the Arab Spring, after the revolution there, made a number of very smart decisions about how they were going to work together—exactly the same kind of initiative that we would like to see the Libyans demonstrate in terms of their own transition.

Mr. BERA. Great. Thank you.

Ms. ROS-LEHTINEN. Thank you, Dr. Bera. Dr. Yoho.

Mr. YOHO. Thank you, Madam Chair.

Sir, I appreciate you being here. You know, I always get a kick out of you guys when you come in and we talk about promoting democracy over there and, you know, if you look at the traditional democracies they only last about 200 years, and a democracy is mob rule. It is majority rule.

The thing that has worked with our country is it is a constitutional republic—that we go through a democratic process to elect leaders—and, you know, when we look at the history of these democracies, we are trying to promote something that is unsustainable because they always fall into decay and it has been proven over and over in history.

So I hope we change that dynamic. With saying that, you know, when I look at what we have done in the Middle East over the last 40 or 50 years, you know, we have spent over—we have invested over $78 billion in Egypt, you know, and they are struggling now, and the other countries that we have entered we have seen them struggling.

One of my questions is how effective is the U.N. Security Council in initiating and carrying out the cease fire that they brokered at the end of August? I mean, do you see that as something that is going to hold?

Is it going to be effective and is it going to lead to some stability in that country? We have seen it so many times where they go in there and just—it decays, and the thing that made our democracy work, our republic work, is we had a group of people that laid everything on the line to fight for freedom and liberty.

Do they have that same sentiment? So go back to the U.N. first. Do you see them initiating and carrying this out to be effective? Go ahead and answer that first.

Mr. FEIERSTEIN. Congressman, first, let me say I couldn't agree with you more that, really, the ability to sustain democratic governance is really based on the stability of the institutions that support it and then the reason—I mean, we can talk about the reason that the U.S. has been successful that way is because we had strong institutions that managed and guided that democracy and kept it from deteriorating into mob rule.

Where we are right now, of course, is that we have a new SRSG—Senior Representative for the Secretary General, Bernardino Leon, who has just taken over from Tarek Mitri as the U.N. representative for Libya.

He has visited Libya over the last several days and held talks with a number of the leading Libyan politicians and is working very hard with our support and with the support of the rest of the international community to try to get the violence to stop and to move into that political dialogue.

Mr. YOHO. Okay. And then right now how effective or successful will Khalifa Haftar be, in your opinion, since he has an anti-Islamist view, versus the people that are fighting that are of the more Islamic, maybe radical view?

Do you see that being successful, you know, because you have got a divergence of ideologies and what we have seen developing in Turkey and what you have seen developing in Qatar, you know, those people are standing—like Turkey realizes they can't survive without being a Muslim Islamist state, and when you have somebody that is trying to develop that in Libya, I just see that as a no-win. What is your opinion on that?

Mr. FEIERSTEIN. Sir, I think that Khalifa Haftar actually put his finger on something that was of concern to a great number of Libyans, which was the drift of the country toward an Islamist agenda, and I think he was successful at that. But, unfortunately, his solution—his channel has been a violent one.

He has pursued a very aggressive stance toward some of these groups and he has ended up promoting a more polarized society and in fact has led to the reaction to his position and that has contributed directly to the violence.

Mr. YOHO. Let me interrupt you here because I am about out of time. You said the country was drifting to the Islamist view and he stopped that.

If it is drifting that way, is that not public sentiment of what they want and so there is going to be resentment and there is going to be that internal conflict? I don't see—I don't see a good solution in that.

Mr. FEIERSTEIN. And this is exactly right—that there are differences of view within that society. There are some people who are supporting a more Islamic vision for their future and there are some who are more secular.

So and, again, we believe that the important thing is that there are elements on both sides of that divide who are committed to a democratic future, who are committed to a more open tolerant society. We want to support them.

Khalifa Haftar, unfortunately, has deepened the polarization in the society through violence and has deepened the divisions and made it more difficult to reach a political negotiated solution.

Mr. YOHO. Okay. Thank you.

Ms. ROS-LEHTINEN. Thank you, Dr. Yoho. Mr. Connolly of Virginia.

Mr. CONNOLLY. Thank you, Madam Chairman.

Mr. Ambassador, in your testimony—in your written statement you refer to the fact that our Embassy has been relocated to Malta. So what is its mission? How does it function? Malta is not that far away but it ain't in Libya.

Mr. FEIERSTEIN. Absolutely. The good thing, of course, obviously, our intention is to get back to Libya as soon as the security circumstances permit.

Mr. CONNOLLY. So the purpose of relocation was a security purpose?

Mr. FEIERSTEIN. The reason that we withdrew from Tripoli in the first place was because there was fighting in the area, immediately around the Embassy to the point where the security of our personnel was in danger. Their ability to move around and do their jobs was very, very limited.

Mr. CONNOLLY. Well, let me—let me ask about that. I get the point. Even from Malta, is there a central governor? Are there ministers to whom they can relate and do their job?

Mr. FEIERSTEIN. Yes, sir. Ambassador Jones is able on the phone and also in person—because many of the Libyan leaders come through Malta on a regular basis and so she has been able to meet with the foreign minister.

She has been able to meet with the prime minister. She was here during the Africa summit and participated in all those conversations.

Mr. CONNOLLY. But let me—but I guess what I am getting at is it is not just our functionality but the functionality of the counterpart. I mean, to what extent would it be fair to say that is all mythology? I mean, yeah, they may have that title but they are not functioning as the minister of foreign affairs.

You know, it is almost a Potemkin government, given the role of the militias, given recent history in Tripoli in terms of a takeover of the city for a while by an Islamist-oriented militia.

What are we—I mean, are we going through sort of the motions of diplomacy as if we are dealing with a real structured government when in fact we are not?

Mr. FEIERSTEIN. No, sir. I think—first of all, of course, Ambassador Jones is able to be in touch with a broad spectrum of political leaders in Libya—not just the government, not just the prime minister but across the board. So she is able to carry out our efforts to mediate, to promote political resolutions, to try to bring the parties together.

Mr. CONNOLLY. What is it you think is the critical sine qua non for trying to see a functioning government, if not a stable government, emerge from this morass?

Mr. FEIERSTEIN. The sine qua non would be, one, an end to violence; two, we would like to see full participation in the House of Representatives, which is the Libyan Parliament.

Mr. CONNOLLY. We Democrats would like to see that here in our House of Representatives as well.

Mr. FEIERSTEIN. And, three, of course, we would like to see the formation of a new government in Libya that would reflect fairly the full spectrum of political representation inside the House of Representatives. And so——

Mr. CONNOLLY. Wouldn't that be an Islamicist-dominated legislature, though, if it did what you just said—only represented a spectrum of opinion?

Mr. FEIERSTEIN. No, sir. I think that if you look at the election of the House of Representatives in June, it was a fairly good cross section of what we consider to be the entire political spectrum. Most of the members are independents and we believe that it is a fair representation of the Libyan population.

Mr. CONNOLLY. So that is a hopeful analysis. Final question, because I am going to run out of time, one of our goals is to create a General Purpose Force. Is that correct?

And the reason for that, obviously, is to substitute that ordered government force for roving militias, some of which may have good intentions, some of which may have an agenda with which we would disagree. But you can't have a stable functioning government if you don't have the ability to police in a normal functioning way.

What are the prospects for us to succeed in training 5,000 to 8,000 members of the GPF and to have it hold together and not, you know, disintegrate as we have seen in some other countries?

Mr. FEIERSTEIN. That is absolutely still our objective. As I mentioned earlier, the Libyans have now signed the letter of agreement that would allow us to go forward. There is still the funding issue that we are waiting to resolve.

But as soon as the security conditions permit, we continue to hold out as our objective to set up that force and to see it take on its responsibilities for security in the country.

Mr. CONNOLLY. Thank you, Madam Chairman. My time is up.

Ms. ROS-LEHTINEN. Thank you very much, sir.

Mr. Perry is recognized.

Mr. PERRY. Thank you, Madam Chairman, and thank you, Ambassador. I got to tell you, while I listened to your testimony I feel like I am living in some kind of twilight zone of altered reality here.

You know, even when you just speak of the last questioners—you know, how do we expect to train these folks—and you say well, we have an agreement with the Libyans to do this, and I am thinking, you know, we have an—there is all these militias.

They are having, essentially, a civil war. Like, what agreement do we have and have you ever tried to train troops under fire? I mean, it sounds—it sounds patently absurd. Let me just ask you this.

You know, articles in the New Yorker and the Washington Post essentially said that the administration has a policy regarding Libya in particular and, in my opinion, in many other things of leading from behind.

Assuming maybe that has some truth or not to it, in your opinion, first of all, is there any truth to that? Is there any—have we led from behind?

Mr. FEIERSTEIN. Sir, I think that if you look at the history of our engagement with Libya since 2011, since the uprising against Muammar Gaddafi, you will see that the United States has been extremely engaged, beginning in September 2011 with Secretary Clinton's leadership at a meeting in Paris.

Mr. PERRY. But forgive me for interrupting. Engaged is one thing. Leading is another. Leading is a whole different paradigm.

So are we engaged or are we leading? And for leading show me or demonstrate—display to me how the oversight of our leadership has contributed to the success or the failure of what has happened in Libya.

Mr. FEIERSTEIN. What I would say, sir, is that the United States remains the focal point—it remains the center of gravity for the international community.

When the United States stands up and demonstrates resolve and demonstrates direction, the international community generally supports and falls into place behind. And so I think in the case of Libya, if you are looking at what we have tried to do in terms of promoting democracy and governance, building institutional capacity, addressing some of the security issues through the General Purpose Force and as well as border security and some of the other activities, I think those are all areas where the United States has played a leadership role in coordinating and bringing together the full international community.

I think that in the—in the period immediately before Ramadan, right after the elections in June, you saw the United States with our friends and partners in the international community working very aggressively, trying to work out—the chairwoman mentioned the 10-point plan.

We were very much involved in developing and negotiating that 10-point plan with the Libyans. So I think over and over again you see a——

Mr. PERRY. Well, let me offer this conjecture. With all due respect to the administration and the State Department, if it is as you say, that we are leading and the international coalition is behind us, that this is a breathtaking failure at this point. And I don't know how it is going to end up but at this moment it seems like a breathtaking failure of leadership and actualization and implementation.

I mean, I look at 110, 111 EU personnel charged with securing the border and I look at the size of the border of—you know, I don't know what kind of program anybody is on that think that that is going to work.

But to me just simple arithmetic says that it has no absolutely—it is preposterous. That having been said, you know, I think about some of the other comments that have been made here regarding programs and sanctions.

Do you think that rebel forces fighting one another with heavy weapons that they have procured from the failed state care about sanctions? And what programs are working under the auspices of, you know, thousands and hundreds of thousands of displaced civilians trying to live among, you know, a war-tattered country and a war zone with foreign fighters coming in and arms coming in and going out?

I mean, that is this altered state of reality that I feel like I am hearing here, and you say if we—if we can stabilize. We are not stabilizing anything.

We are sitting here watching this thing burn down and we are milling around with all these foolish policies that we can't implement and we can't expect them to implement because there is no governance there.

I mean, I am sorry but that is—I am listening to this rhetoric here and it sounds like a bunch of mumbo jumbo that means nothing on the ground. Am I wrong?

Mr. FEIERSTEIN. Sir, I don't want to underestimate the challenges that are in front of us and, of course, they are huge and it is a very difficult environment in which we are trying to work.

But the fact of the matter is that there are opportunities. The EUBAM mission that you mentioned, the border assistance mission, is not to guard the border but to train the Libyans to take on that responsibility themselves and at the end of the day the Libyans are going to be responsible for what happens in their country and they are going to have to do these things.

So we can work with them. We can help them. We can support them. I think that many of the programs that we are—that we are pursuing now, particularly on the governance side—trying to build institutional capacity—are things that are going to succeed over time.

But there is no—there is no getting around the basic point that you are making, I think, which is that this is an extremely difficult and challenging environment at this time. We need to stick with it.

We need to try to push through this particular period and to get the Libyans into a situation where many of the things that we are trying to accomplish actually become effective and implementable.

Ms. ROS-LEHTINEN. Thank you very much. Thank you, Mr. Perry.

Mr. Kennedy of Massachusetts.

Mr. KENNEDY. Thank you, Madame Chair. Mr. Ambassador, thank you very much for your service. Thank you for your testimony today.

A couple of points that I would love to get your clarification on or just flush out to the extent that you can in this setting, sir. First off, as you have just indicated, the situation on the ground in Libya is very complex and very complicated, going to take a period of time.

We are seeing instability throughout and a failure of institutions throughout and governing institutions throughout the Middle East and other parts of the world as well. This is not a short-term solution.

Do you have—are you comfortable giving any sort of ball park assessment? Is this months? Is this years? Is this a decade? What type of forecast are we looking for—are we looking at here, to the best you can assess at the moment?

Mr. FEIERSTEIN. Mr. Kennedy, I must say that it is something when I was in Yemen we had the same question. We dealt with the same things. To be entirely honest, I think that this is a very long-term investment of time and effort and energy.

The fact is that we are dealing with a society here that had no institutional capacity, that had no governing capacity, and so if we are going to succeed it is going to require a very long-term effort on the part of the Libyans primarily, of course, but also with the support of the international community.

Mr. KENNEDY. And, Ambassador, I know there was some talk a few moments ago about some of the weapons that, at this point, are rampant throughout Libya.

To the extent that you can say and can say in this setting, are you aware of any of those weapons being transferred through the Sinai into either—into Gaza or into other settings that are being used to basically foment violence in Israel and the surrounding areas, or into Syria, for that matter?

Mr. FEIERSTEIN. I couldn't say specifically that I know whether they are going to Gaza. I can say that the concern about the flow of weapons out of Libya into other troubled regions—into Syria, Iraq or potentially into Gaza or the Sinai—is something that we do watch very carefully and we are very concerned about.

We actually have, with the support of the Congress and based on congressional appropriations, we actually have a very aggressive program of trying to recover a lot of these conventional weapons.

We have, for example, secured over 5,000 MANPADS that were in Libya. So we are working to try to dry up that resource and also, of course, the new U.N. Security Council Resolution 2174 strengthened the arms embargo on Libya so that we are not seeing a lot of weapons coming in.

Mr. KENNEDY. And, Mr. Ambassador, I apologize if I am going to ask you to repeat something. But given, as you just forecasted, the length of the commitment, the challenge that you are—you have outlined, this is not something, I don't think, the United States can do alone.

Clearly, as you indicated, this is going to be the responsibility primarily of Libyans but there is evidence, certainly, at least from the U.S. press that there is other nations that have been involved military in this conflict.

What is the appetite of other nations in the Middle East or the surrounding nations there to actually help sustain—to build up some of the civil society there?

This is not something that the United States is going to be able to have the deciding outcome nor should we be, I think, rebuilding an entire Libyan state. We have tried that once recently.

Mr. FEIERSTEIN. Absolutely, and I think that there is a broad agreement between the United States, the United Nations, of course, our friends in the European Union as well as in the region about what kind of society we would like to see emerge in Libya.

We may not always agree on the tactics but I think that we agree on the end state and I think that some of the Gulf States, the Emiratis and some of the others, are absolutely willing and committed to contributing to that.

Mr. KENNEDY. The type of commitment, sir, that would actually get us to where we need to go or where you believe we need to— we need to get to?

I mean, the resources, whether it is military troops, civil society funding that is going to be necessary to build up a functioning government in Libya, is massive and that is—I hesitate to believe that we here in the United States are going to appropriate the sufficient funding to do that.

I hesitate to believe that other nations in the region are going to hesitate to do that and if they are not then we are going to be looking at a series of instability for or a sequence of instability for an awfully long time.

Is there a commitment from other countries to actually do this or to do it in a very real way or to just see what happens?

Mr. FEIERSTEIN. Well, I think one thing—one point to make, of course, is that Libya is not a poor country and so a lot of the funding, a lot of the investment for these changes can come directly from the Libyans.

I think in terms of institutional capacity building, the United States, along with our partners in the European Union primarily, are committed to taking on this—taking on this obligation, this commitment to work with the Libyans to try to achieve that.

I think also we can work with some of our friends in the Gulf. Secretary Kerry is going to be meeting with the group that includes our European as well as our—GCC and the Turks in New York in 2 weeks to have exactly these kinds of conversations.

Mr. KENNEDY. Thank you, Mr. Ambassador. Madame Chair, thank you for the extra time.

Ms. ROS-LEHTINEN. Thank you, Mr. Kennedy. One of our many wonderful vets serving on our committee, Mr. Kinzinger, is recognized.

Mr. KINZINGER. Thank you, Madam Chair, and thank you, Ambassador, for being here. I am going to say on the outset I was a supporter of intervention in Libya. I thought we did the right thing.

I have, obviously, been very disappointed with the follow through and what it looks like today and I think it is important to kind of discover, as we are having this hearing, you know, what a post-war looks like, especially as, you know, what appears likely there will be intervention in Syria and there are questions, rightly, about what Syria looks like post-Assad which, hopefully, there is a post-Assad time in Syria.

I am sure it has probably already been touched on when I wasn't here but, you know, the idea of leading from behind—and I know that is something that has haunted the administration. They probably wish they never would have said it.

But I think it is a reality and something that, you know, is smart to understand that, you know, America does best when it leads from the front and when America understands and, frankly, I don't know why that is something we are ashamed of.

I mean, we ought to be very proud of the fact that if there is a problem in the world people look not to Russia, not to China, not to chaos. They look to the United States, and while we can't do everything, I like to be in that position.

I like to be in the position where people look at us as a force for good and a force for stability. So anyway, that said, as the war raged, Gaddafi was killed and we saw a post-war.

Where I found a lot of concerns was in terms of being able to build maybe a NATO mission afterwards or even a short time period that the United Nations mission lasted. So let me ask you a bit about the U.N. mission.

Why was the UNSMIL's mandate only for 3 months and then it was extended for an additional 3 months? Did the administration insist on a longer mandate tied to goals and objectives rather than an arbitrary time line?

I was just in Liberia, for instance, and that has been a mission that is successful but it is, obviously, quite ongoing.

Mr. FEIERSTEIN. Sir, I believe that the mission was organized initially for 3 months and then an additional 3 months, as you said. My understanding is that that is not uncommon for these kinds of missions to get that done.

Since March 2012, it has now been rolled over each time for a 1-year period. So after the initial start-up, we have moved into a more stable annual review.

Mr. KINZINGER. And do you think the administration was being overly optimistic or unrealistic in its assertion of the Libyan—the capacity of the Libyan Government and what accounts for the administration's misunderstanding of the commitment needed to assist the Libyan transition?

And I don't mean that accusatorialy but was it just we maybe thought they could get their act together faster or what was it?

Mr. FEIERSTEIN. I think that is absolutely a fair question and I would say that in all fairness probably there was an optimism, an over optimism perhaps, not only on the part of the United States but also on the part of the Libyans themselves and I think that it took a little bit of time before people realized really how weak the institutions were inside of Libya and how serious the internal divisions were so that as we moved along, remembering, of course, that initially the Libyans themselves did not want the foreign intervention.

They didn't want a lot of engagement on the part of the international community and it was really only as these—the situation became clearer did they begin to turn to the international community and did we begin to respond.

Mr. KINZINGER. And I think that is a fair point. Is that the same—why would the—how come the U.N. was not given a peace-keeping mandate?

You know, if you look at, for instance, our experience in Kosovo with KFOR and the NATO model engagement there, I mean, it seems to be that, I think, is largely seen as a very successful mission.

What is the reason? Is it the Libyans' request? What was it that we didn't implement something like that? Is it a lack of will on our side? Was it the lack of will on our NATO partners? I think that is important, again, especially as we look to Syria and the future there.

Mr. FEIERSTEIN. I think that very clearly the Libyans themselves said that they would not welcome or support a peacekeeping mission.

Mr. KINZINGER. Do you think there would have been—let us say the Libyan—I know we are playing games, in essence, in asking this but had the Libyans said we need a peacekeeping force here, do you think there was the will not just in the United States but in Europe to provide that?

Mr. FEIERSTEIN. It is a hypothetical question, of course——

Mr. KINZINGER. Right.

Mr. FEIERSTEIN [continuing]. Hard to answer, but I believe that there would have been interest had that been a request from the Libyans.

In fairness, of course, we have seen some talk in recent days and weeks about some kind of an international stabilization force and I can tell you that Secretary Kerry is very interested in exploring that, although the divisions within Libya are still an obstacle and still may prevent something like that from happening.

Mr. KINZINGER. Good. And that is where I was going to go with that and I appreciate it. Thank you for your service. Thank you for being here, and I yield back.

Ms. ROS-LEHTINEN. Thank you very much, sir. Mr. Lowenthal of California.

Mr. LOWENTHAL. Thank you. As someone who is not on the African Subcommittee and new to the Congress and learning about Libya, this is a very depressing hearing, you know, and I am not pointing fingers.

I am not saying anything that we have done. It is just I am not sure I understand what a country—if this is a country on the brink of a failed state what a failed state would look like—I mean, this seems to me.

So I want to—before I ask you something I want to state two things. One is I want to follow up on something that the ranking member, Mr. Deutch, said.

I would like to have a classified hearing. I would like to know what that role has been in terms of the Egyptians and just what the United States knew about that and understood about that. That is one, and also, I too would—while you lay out, and I think it is a very positive thing, a potential dialogue on how we could bring people together and how the Libyans—there is tremendous potential—it still eludes me how we get there and that leads to my question.

Could you give me—maybe others know—a little bit more detailed explanation of who are—what are the political factions that you have mentioned?

What are the militias? Can—you know, can you tell us a little bit more about what is really there today and what exists and who is the most powerful?

Mr. FEIERSTEIN. Well, a lot of the militias, of course, Mr. Lowenthal, are a holdover from the resistance to Muammar Gaddafi. So the two—the two militias that you talk about mostly in terms of Tripoli are the Misratans and the Zintan.

Those are two towns inside of Libya, Misrata and Zintan, and they both had militias that fought against Gaddafi in 2011, and since 2011 they have kept the militias together. They have occupied various parts of Tripoli.

The Zintan were the ones who were in control of Tripoli International Airport and the conflict that erupted in Tripoli a couple of months ago, which eventually led to the departure of American diplomats as well as most of the other diplomats in the city and most of the foreign community, were clashes between the Misratans and the Zintan.

Now, you know, and we need—because there is not a clear hard line and as I tried to say earlier on, I think that on both sides of the political divide within Libya you see different gradations, different ideas.

And so although the Misratans tend toward the more Islamist side, that does not mean that they are Islamists—that they are hardcore Muslim fundamentalists.

But they tend that way, and the Zintan tend more toward the secular side. But that doesn't necessarily mean that they are entirely, you know, liberal democrats. They have various gradations also.

So you see a number of different elements. And then, of course, you have Khalifa Haftar, who emerged in the area around Benghazi who also has been extremely active and pushed what he calls Operation Dignity, which he claimed was a move toward defending secular elements, secular ideas inside of Libya, which struck a very positive chord with many Libyans but also, as I mentioned earlier, because he has chosen a violent path has deepened the polarization in the society.

Mr. LOWENTHAL. Is there any one group that is on the ascendency?

Mr. FEIERSTEIN. The Misratans have fundamentally succeeded in eliminating Zintan control inside of Tripoli but, overall, our assessment is that none of the actors inside of Libya have the capacity or the ability to succeed militarily.

We think, at the end of the day, that the forces are roughly in balance so that they could not win an outright victory.

Mr. LOWENTHAL. Thank you, and I yield back.

Chairman ROYCE. Thank you. We go now to Mr. Ron DeSantis of Florida.

Mr. DESANTIS. Thank you, Mr. Chairman, and thanks to the Ambassador for coming. I am glad we are examining this because I think and, understandably, a lot of the focus of both the media and our time in Congress focuses on what is happening with ISIS, the

Gaza-Israeli conflict, Iran's pursuit of a nuclear weapon and those are all very, very critical issues.

I think Libya really represents a catastrophic failure in policy. If you look back in 2011, U.S. intervention was really on the side of a lot of these Islamist rebels and I think that that was a cruel lesson that we learned 2 years ago tomorrow when our Ambassador was murdered by Islamic militants in Benghazi.

Simply removing a dictator, no matter how unsavory that individual is, is not, in this part of this world, going to lead necessarily to anything better and it can actually sometimes lead to more chaos.

In our policy we need to reorient it so that we are vindicating our national interest but doing it in a way where we are skewing, trying to socially engineer these societies.

It is just beyond our capacity to do. I think it is—I think it creates a lot of unintended consequences. And so if you look today, seems to me that there are far more Islamic jihadists operating not only in Libya but in North Africa today than there was prior to the intervention in 2011.

But that will be a question I ask to you. Do you acknowledge that today there are more Islamic militants that are armed and operating inside of Libya than there were prior to 2011?

Mr. FEIERSTEIN. It is a hard question to answer. Let me make a few points, if I may, sir. One, of course, is that the reason that the United States and the international community intervened in 2011 was because of the brutality of the Gaddafi regime's——

Mr. DESANTIS. Well, that was the posited initial reason but that, surely, and I think you would have to acknowledge that very quickly evolved into a regime change mission.

I mean, that may have been the initial pretext. But listen, and I appreciate you wanting to clarify that. I do have a few other questions.

I don't want—I just don't want to relitigate that. I was just setting up kind of my posture on it just for the record and I appreciate you wanting to engage.

But since my time is limited, can you just speak to the number of militants? Do you think that there are more terrorists operating in Libya today than there were prior to 2011?

Mr. FEIERSTEIN. And, again, and I appreciate that and the specific—the specific answer is that it is very hard to say because al-Qaeda and the Islamic Maghreb is not new and is not a result of 2011. It was there many years ago.

We know that there was a brutal war inside of Algeria for a number of years in the 1990s which was driven by Islamic extremism in that society and so those people were there and that has been a factor in North Africa for many, many years.

So this is a longstanding challenge. I think that the concern that we have and maybe the concern that you are touching on is the fact that Libya is an ungoverned space now and so that there is an ability of these organizations and these groups to operate in Libya in a way that they perhaps couldn't before.

Mr. DESANTIS. Do you—understanding that and I agree, the administration is proposing to lift longstanding restrictions on Libyan nationals conducting flight training and nuclear training in the United States.

Given this fact that you have acknowledged, doesn't that seem like an odd time to want to do that, given that we know there are Libyans inside of Libya who are very much hostile to the United States?

Mr. FEIERSTEIN. Sir, I think and, of course, this is an issue for the Department of Homeland Security, but we support the lifting of that because Libya is the only country in the world on which that restriction is applied, including countries that are designated as state sponsors of terrorism, don't have that restriction applied to them.

And even if we lift that particular restriction, of course, Libyans who are coming or applying to come here would still be subject to all of the regular safeguards that we would apply to any visa applicant.

Mr. DESANTIS. Let me ask you this, a final—my time is close to being expired. President el-Sisi of Egypt has really been strong to target Islamic groups in Egypt and throughout the region and, of course, there are the reports that Egypt conducted air strikes along with the United Arab Emirates. Seems to me that a lot of the Islamist groups they try to appeal for outside help to Turkey and Qatar. So what is the administration's position?

Are we firmly in the side—on the side of Egypt and the UAE and do we recognize that Turkey and Qatar are not playing a constructive role in Libya or are we aligning ourselves differently?

Mr. FEIERSTEIN. The position that we have taken both in public and in private with all of those parties is that we believe that unilateral foreign military intervention in Libya is polarizing in that society, deepens the divisions and makes it more difficult to try to achieve the kind of political way forward. A negotiated solution to these differences that, in our view, is the only way that we are going to resolve this problem inside of Libya.

So we are opposed to all outside intervention that supports any faction in its pursuit of a violent outcome to the situation there.

Mr. DESANTIS. My time has expired and I yield back.

Chairman ROYCE. Karen Bass of Los Angeles, California.

Ms. BASS. Thank you, and thank you, Mr. Ambassador, for clarifying our original reason for intervening in Libya. I think sometimes when groups come to our attention here we think they might be emerging for the first time.

You know, an example is Boko Haram. We heard of Boko Haram for the first time but we know Boko Haram has been around for a long time. I wouldn't want it left that we intervened on behalf of Islamic jihadists.

But I did want you to address the regional implications because part of what my colleague was saying, you know, certainly was accurate. I think of the coup that happened in Mali and its direct relationship to the destabilization in Libya.

So I wanted to know if maybe you could give me an update on what is happening in Niger and Chad that might be related to Libya.

Mr. FEIERSTEIN. Well, we are very concerned, of course, on precisely this issue of the potential bleed over of instability in Libya to all of its neighbors and, certainly, we have had a number of conversations with the Tunisians, who are very concerned, as well as the countries of the Sahel.

During the Africa Summit, Undersecretary Sherman actually had a session on security in the Maghreb and the Sahel that discussed many of these issues and, you know, one of the things that we are trying to do is to build up border security and the capacity of those states to prevent the bleed-out of instability in Libya into their societies and that would affect the stability of those countries.

So we have the Trans-Sahel Counterterrorism Program. We have a number of other initiatives that will help address border security and, of course, more broadly we have a number of counterterrorism initiatives and other initiatives in the Sahel region to help build up the security and stability of those societies.

Ms. BASS. You know, do you know what has happened to the— there were many sub-Saharan Africans that were in Libya that, right after Gaddafi fell, came under some brutal repression by a variety of the militia forces, and do you know the status of those groups—whether they were able to safely leave Libya?

Are they still there? Are they still going through what they were going through after the fall of Gaddafi?

Mr. FEIERSTEIN. Ma'am, I am sorry. I remember the situation very well. I don't know the answer to your question but will be happy to get the answer and get it back to you.

Ms. BASS. All right. I would appreciate that. And then I am not sure if this has come up before but understanding what has happened in Tripoli, what is the status of the airport now?

Mr. FEIERSTEIN. The status of the airport is that it is still closed. We believe it has been heavily damaged and that it will require a great deal of reconstruction once the situation stabilizes.

Ms. BASS. Are there planes that the militia groups have access to?

Mr. FEIERSTEIN. No, ma'am. We have seen the reports. There were some assertions that 11 planes had been taken from the airport. We have actually had an opportunity to examine that issue and we can say categorically that that is absolutely without foundation.

Ms. BASS. Gaddafi's son?

Mr. FEIERSTEIN. Another question I am going to have to take back and get back to you.

Ms. BASS. Okay. All right. Thank you. I yield.

Chairman ROYCE. Okay. Ms. Tulsi Gabbard of Hawaii.

Ms. GABBARD. Thank you very much, Mr. Chairman.

Mr. Ambassador, I appreciate you spending your time here with us this morning. Do you have any State Department personnel left in Libya?

Mr. FEIERSTEIN. No, ma'am.

Ms. GABBARD. It is—I have got a couple of questions here. I will try to get through them quickly. There have been some different references to the fighting forces on the ground in Libya. Some are calling them rival militias.

There has been some talk of a sectarian civil war, others of Islamic extremists of varying names, whether they are al-Qaeda or other—go by other names. Which is it?

Is it Islamic extremists who are trying to take over territory? My understanding is that this isn't a sectarian civil war necessarily, and how would you characterize it?

Mr. FEIERSTEIN. I think that that is absolutely correct, although as I mentioned earlier, the different groups have different colorations in terms of where they fall on the political spectrum. Some are more secular.

Some are more Islamist. But it is not necessarily a sectarian conflict. Our view is that primarily it is a fight for power and for resources and for influence.

Ms. GABBARD. I think it is difficult to see any so-called political solution on the horizon, given the situation on the ground, given there is no State Department personnel, and I see from what occurred since 2011 with the lack of governance there that, really, as has been noted earlier today, change needs to come from the Libyan people, that we don't have a good track record of nation building in other countries and that this needs to occur organically within that country.

AFRICOM commander—U.S. AFRICOM Commander General Rodriguez recently warned that al-Qaeda adherents and affiliates there in Libya are gaining strength as "arms, ammunition, explosives from Libya continue to move throughout the region in northwest Africa," and others within the Department of Defense have stated that if this situation is left unchecked then we will continue to see the threat to the United States and our interests heightened as we are seeing in other areas in the Middle East. What are we doing to prevent that?

Mr. FEIERSTEIN. Well, I think that, again, all of the programs that we have—I think that your basic point is exactly the right one, which is that this is something that the solutions need to come organically from inside of Libya from the Libyan people, and actually we are seeing some positive signs that there is a dialogue going on among the Libyan people that we hope would lead to some kind of a political path forward.

It is nascent, it is very low key, but it is there and we believe that over time hopefully the Libyans on both sides of the political spectrum, on all sides of the political spectrum, will actually come together and agree on a dialogue, agree on a negotiation.

That is the only way that we are going to be able to get past this period of militias and the violence and get into a situation where we can begin to work on some of the institutional capacity building on the security side as well as the governance side that, over the long term, will resolve those issues and resolve our concerns.

Ms. GABBARD. Wouldn't you say as that dialogue and those conversations are going on, though, that you have these Islamic extremists who are continuing to gain strength in the region, not only affecting Libya but others?

Mr. FEIERSTEIN. It is a concern without doubt and again, I think that over the long term, although we in the international community can help and we will help in institutional capacity, but our view is that the vast majority of the Libyan people don't want that.

They don't support that kind of a vision, and that if we have viable governing institutions—if the House of Representatives gains traction, if we see broad participation in that and the creation of a government that fairly represents the various elements in the House of Representatives that the Libyan people will rally around and that the Islamic extremists in that society are relatively small and can be managed and eliminated.

Ms. GABBARD. Thank you. My concern directly is in how this—how they and how this affects our interests—the interests of the United States, the safety of the American people.

It wasn't very long ago that ISIS was determined to be a very so-called small threat that didn't need to be taken seriously and, obviously, we are seeing that that is not the case.

So our targeting and our concern with these Islamic extremists there needs to be in a broader vision of recognizing that this isn't about a specific country whether it is Libya or Iraq or Syria.

This is about a greater threat that is posed directly to the American people. Thank you.

Mr. FEIERSTEIN. And we agree with that completely, of course.

Chairman ROYCE. Lois Frankel of Florida.

Ms. FRANKEL. Thank you, Mr. Chair. Let me—let me follow that and I think it is important for the public to understand why we spend our time on these issues.

So I would like you, in 4 minutes and 51 seconds, if you could, tell us what you believe is the strategic importance of Libya and the region, why we intervened and what lessons we have learned.

Mr. FEIERSTEIN. Well, I think that the strategic importance of Libya touches on a number of issues. One, of course, is that Libya is a major provider of energy resources to the world.

Before the 2011 revolution, they were producing about 1½ million barrels of oil a day. They are back now to about 800,000, which is growing by the day.

They are a very important provider of energy to—particularly to Europe and so in terms of the overall global economy, Libya plays a very important role. They are strategically located in the region. They have a long coastline on the Mediterranean.

One of the issues that we have seen, of course, unrelated to the issue of Islamic extremism or security is the flow of immigration and the destabilizing effect that that flow has had on southern Europe because of the inability of Libya to control its borders and to prevent that flow through.

I think that, again, as your colleague mentioned just a moment ago, we have serious concerns about the impact of or the potential impact of Libya as an ungoverned space for groups like al-Qaeda and the Islamic Maghreb, Ansar al-Sharia, which is the group that was responsible for the attack on our facility in Benghazi 2 years ago, to continue to metastasize, to prevent or to pose a threat to its neighbors, to Tunisia, to Algeria, to the states of the Sahel, to Egypt.

Egypt is—has great concerns about the flow or the possible flow of extremists across their border into the western desert of Egypt and so we see that potential, the potential that eventually you might see increasingly a linkage between the extremism inside of Libya with other parts of the Middle East—Syria, Iraq, et cetera—and eventually a threat to security and stability around the world.

And so we have a positive—we have a positive strategic interest, which is in seeing Libya as a secure stable producer of energy resources and an important factor in promoting global economic security, and then there is also the negative impact of an ungoverned Libya and how that might threaten our security.

Ms. FRANKEL. And what lessons have we learned from the intervention and the chaos that we see there now?

Mr. FEIERSTEIN. Well, I think that where we are now is that there is a greater recognition today, I believe, in what kind of challenge we confront inside of Libya and the fact that helping the Libyans move to a secure stable state with capable institutions that can provide basic services to the citizens, that can govern, that can provide security is going to be a long-term challenge which is going to require a long-term commitment on the part of the United States and our partners in the international community to help the Libyans achieve that objective.

Ms. FRANKEL. Thank you, Mr. Chair. I waive the rest of my time.

Chairman ROYCE. Thank you. We go now to Mr. Brad Sherman of California.

Mr. SHERMAN. Thank you. I have sat here in this room while the administration gets berated because somehow you are not able to achieve a loving and peaceful world at—and achieve it without any American casualties.

We don't have control of what is going on on the ground in Syria or Iraq or Libya, and somehow if we only had somebody in the White House with a different personality that everyone in the Middle East would do what we said and we would be in control and we would achieve it all without any troops on the ground.

Are you aware of any strategy that has realistically proposed a method to achieve American leadership from the front, control of what is going on, the destruction of all dangerous evil forces without substantial American casualties?

Have any of the think tanks here in Washington come up with such a ground plan? You could give me a one-word answer.

Mr. FEIERSTEIN. No, sir. I think——

Mr. SHERMAN. Thank you. It is—you know, destroy all dangerous evil is a great slogan. But the real slogan for an effective foreign policy is managing a messy world and I guess you can't—that isn't poetry.

But the fact is that if we wanted an orderly Libya we could, you know, conjecture how many hundreds of casualties a year we would have to suffer to implement that immediately and not by—you know, obviously leading from behind is a terrible slogan but influencing from afar involves a lot fewer casualties than taking control on the ground.

I want to focus a little bit on money. I am the only CPA on this committee, and having already dismissed the idea of glorious slogans, pinch pennies now is probably the least glorious slogan.

But this is a very rich country. American taxpayers have spent billions of dollar to help the Libyan people. Libya acknowledges over $6 billion of debt to bankers, to other governments. Doesn't acknowledge one cent of debt to the United States.

What have we done? I mean, know Libya is supposed to pay for the military training in Bulgaria but it is not happening. We are—the Libyan special operation forces are being trained at the taxpayer expense.

How forceful has the State Department been in saying, you ought to be paying us for the billions of dollars we spent a few years ago and at very minimum the gravy train stops now—if you don't have the cash we will take the notes secured by the oil?

Or is American—the interests of the American taxpayer not high on the list?

Mr. FEIERSTEIN. Sir, I think, as you mentioned, Libya is not a country without resources, although, unfortunately, one of the institutional capacities that they are lacking is the capacity to manage their money.

Mr. SHERMAN. I am not saying these promissory notes would be— well, by today's credit rating agencies they might be given Tri- ple A.

But no sane credit rating agency would give them a Triple A rating. But at least get us something. Have you gotten—do you have the promissory notes that would be paid once Libyan security is reestablished, whenever that happens?

Mr. FEIERSTEIN. I think that, certainly, as we go forward and we begin to discuss these programs and these training initiatives that we would like to do with the Libyans that the issue of paying for it is——

Mr. SHERMAN. Can you go back and get the Libyans to assume financial responsibility for the Libyan Special Operations Forces training going on today? Is that a priority for the State Department?

Mr. FEIERSTEIN. The—on the General Purpose Force having the Libyans——

Mr. SHERMAN. And I am focused on the Libyan Special Operation Forces because that is happening now at taxpayer expense.

Mr. FEIERSTEIN. And, Congressman Sherman, I think that the fundamental point is that what we are doing in Libya now we are doing because we believe that it supports the interests of the American people. So the Libyan Special Operations Forces is precisely aimed at trying to prevent the kind of terrorism——

Mr. SHERMAN. We are selling $11 billion worth of arms to Qatar presumably because we think that is consistent with our foreign policy. I am not so sure it is. We are not giving them away. We sell weapons to Australia. Presumably, that is in our national interest.

So why do you defend giving money to Libya rather than taking promissory notes when it is far more—just as much in our interest to provide weapons and training to Australia or Canada, et cetera?

Do people at the State Department care enough about the taxpayer to at least get promissory notes for what we are providing to Libya now?

Mr. FEIERSTEIN. What we are providing to Libya now we are providing because we believe that it is in the interest of the United States to provide it. We don't provide them with weapons. If they want weapons they purchase them in the same way that the Qataris do.

Mr. SHERMAN. But we charge Australia for training. We charge European—the NATO allies for training. We charge for nonlethal supplies.

Sir, you are hiding behind this idea that it is in our interest so we shouldn't charge for it, which really means the State Department doesn't care about the taxpayer, because every time we provide training and weapons that is consistent with our foreign policy, every time we allow our businesses to do business abroad it is consistent with our national policy, and just saying we are going to give away money because the people we are giving it to are consistent with our foreign policy is basically saying you want to give away money.

I yield back. I hope you will take this message back.

Chairman ROYCE. Let me just close here, if I can, by thanking Ambassador Feierstein for his testimony before our committee this morning. We thank the members, too.

Obviously, Ambassador, you have your hands full. As Mr. Lowenthal on this committee said, it is a depressing situation and as the administration works to get a strategy together, a plan together, we hope you will continue to engage with the committee on that.

At that point, we adjourn for now and thank you again, Ambassador.

Mr. FEIERSTEIN. Thank you, Mr. Chairman.

[Whereupon, at 11:49 a.m., the committee was adjourned.]

APPENDIX

MATERIAL SUBMITTED FOR THE RECORD

FULL COMMITTEE HEARING NOTICE
COMMITTEE ON FOREIGN AFFAIRS
U.S. HOUSE OF REPRESENTATIVES
WASHINGTON, DC 20515-6128

Edward R. Royce (R-CA), Chairman

September 10, 2014

TO: MEMBERS OF THE COMMITTEE ON FOREIGN AFFAIRS

You are respectfully requested to attend an OPEN hearing of the Committee on Foreign Affairs, to be held in Room 2172 of the Rayburn House Office Building (and available live on the Committee website at http://www.ForeignAffairs.house.gov):

DATE: Wednesday, September 10, 2014

TIME: 10:00 a.m.

SUBJECT: Libya's Descent

WITNESS: The Honorable Gerald Feierstein
                   Principal Deputy Assistant Secretary
                   Bureau of Near Eastern Affairs
                   U.S. Department of State

By Direction of the Chairman

The Committee on Foreign Affairs seeks to make its facilities accessible to persons with disabilities. If you are in need of special accommodations, please call 202/225-5021 at least four business days in advance of the event, whenever practicable. Questions with regard to special accommodations in general (including availability of Committee materials in alternative formats and assistive listening devices) may be directed to the Committee.

COMMITTEE ON FOREIGN AFFAIRS
MINUTES OF FULL COMMITTEE HEARING

Day___ *Wednesday*___ Date_____ *09/10/14*_____ Room_____ *2172*_____

Starting Time _*10:04 a.m.*_ Ending Time _*11:49 a.m.*_

Recesses |_*0*_| (____to ____) (____to ____) (____to ____) (____to ____) (____to ____) (____to ____)

Presiding Member(s)

Edward R. Royce, Chairman
Rep. Ileana Ros-Lehtinen

Check all of the following that apply:

Open Session ☑   Electronically Recorded (taped) ☑
Executive (closed) Session ☐   Stenographic Record ☑
Televised ☑

TITLE OF HEARING:

Libya's Descent

COMMITTEE MEMBERS PRESENT:

See Attendance Sheet.

NON-COMMITTEE MEMBERS PRESENT:

None.

HEARING WITNESSES: Same as meeting notice attached? Yes ☑ No ☐
(If "no", please list below and include title, agency, department, or organization.)

STATEMENTS FOR THE RECORD: *(List any statements submitted for the record.)*

Rep. Gerald E. Connolly

TIME SCHEDULED TO RECONVENE _____
or
TIME ADJOURNED _*11:49 a.m.*_

Jean Marter, Director of Committee Operations

HOUSE COMMITTEE ON FOREIGN AFFAIRS
FULL COMMITTEE HEARING

PRESENT	MEMBER
X	Edward R. Royce, CA
X	Christopher H. Smith, NJ
X	Ileana Ros-Lehtinen, FL
	Dana Rohrabacher, CA
	Steve Chabot, OH
	Joe Wilson, SC
	Michael T. McCaul, TX
X	Ted Poe, TX
X	Matt Salmon, AZ
	Tom Marino, PA
	Jeff Duncan, SC
X	Adam Kinzinger, IL
X	Mo Brooks, AL
X	Tom Cotton, AR
	Paul Cook, CA
	George Holding, NC
X	Randy K. Weber, Sr., TX
X	Scott Perry, PA
	Steve Stockman, TX
X	Ron DeSantis, FL
	Doug Collins, GA
	Mark Meadows, NC
X	Ted S. Yoho, FL
	Sean Duffy, WI
	Curt Clawson, FL

PRESENT	MEMBER
	Eliot L. Engel, NY
	Eni F.H. Faleomavaega, AS
X	Brad Sherman, CA
	Gregory W. Meeks, NY
	Albio Sires, NJ
X	Gerald E. Connolly, VA
X	Theodore E. Deutch, FL
	Brian Higgins, NY
X	Karen Bass, CA
	William Keating, MA
	David Cicilline, RI
	Alan Grayson, FL
	Juan Vargas, CA
	Bradley S. Schneider, IL
X	Joseph P. Kennedy III, MA
X	Ami Bera, CA
X	Alan S. Lowenthal, CA
	Grace Meng, NY
X	Lois Frankel, FL
X	Tulsi Gabbard, HI
	Joaquin Castro, TX

Statement for the Record
Submitted by Mr. Connolly of Virginia

When the Subcommittee on the Middle East and North Africa held a June hearing to discuss the situation in Libya, many of us voiced concern about a burgeoning militia movement that threatened Libya's already fragile domestic institutions. While cautious optimism was expressed regarding the June 25 elections for Libya's parliament, commonly referred to as its House of Representatives (HOR), concern remained that violence would destabilize Libya's democratic transition.

Specifically, questions were raised about the United States' commitment to training a General Purpose Force (GPF) of 5,000 – 8,000 Libyan military personnel at a joint U.S.-Bulgarian training facility. The plan called for the U.S. to carry out the training in concert with U.S. allies, the United Kingdom, Italy, and Turkey. A parallel effort by our allies would augment the force with 7,000 additional personnel.

The Department of Defense and Libya's then Prime Minister Ali Zeidan conceived and developed this proposal in the spring of last year. However, this was before General Khalifa Belqassem Haftar launched his offensive against militia groups termed "Operation Restore Libyan Dignity" and before the militias had begun to operate in much of the country with impunity. With governing institutions still weak and an emerging and widespread armed conflict on the ground, the specific concern expressed at our June hearing was that the Department of Defense should have an eye towards how a GPF ultimately would be managed and deployed. It is certainly not the intention of the U.S. to further enflame domestic conflict by injecting thousands of well-armed and well-trained Libyan military personnel into a situation without assurances that the institution to which they are accountable is stable and sustainable. On the other hand, Libya cannot address its long-term internal stability needs at the whim of militia warlords. I witnessed that challenge firsthand in a CODEL to Libya several years ago. Airport security in Tripoli, at that time, was provided by militias.

One month after our hearing and the Libyan parliamentary elections, the U.S. Embassy in Tripoli was evacuated and closed due to fighting and growing unrest in the capital. The elections did not have a stabilizing effect as was hoped and two competing factions have since formed parallel governments. One led by Omar Hassi is operating out of Tripoli, and the other under Prime Minister Abdullah al Thinni is in Tobruk. A political reconciliation would likely require that the former General National Congress (GNC) reconvene in order to grant legal governing authority to the HOR. However, before that can happen, active HOR members and those elected members who have abstained due to legality concerns will need to conduct an outreach effort to those whom would grant the HOR the legal authority to govern Libya. Further, concerns about recent measures adopted by the HOR and its proximity to General Haftar would need to be resolved.

The Constitutional Assembly should also be supported in its effort to finish drafting a new constitution for a lasting and inclusive democracy in Libya. This is one path leaders can take to establish the capacity to protect vital institutions and provide security for the people of Libya. It would empower moderates interested in working through differences peacefully. It also would encourage foreign partners to help strengthen military and security institutions in a manner that protects hard fought democratic gains and marginalizes radical militias.

I hope that the State Department can share with us specific plans it has to support a political reconciliation and lasting democracy in Libya. I am interested in the international partners with which we share a common cause in our commitment to a political process. The measure passed by the United Nations Security Council calling for an immediate ceasefire and placing sanctions on those who perpetuate violence is a welcome start to coordinated action in Libya. It is doubtful that continued foreign military intervention would promote the moderation, stability and peace, much less the government, Libyans want.

www.ingramcontent.com/pod-product-compliance
Lightning Source LLC
Chambersburg PA
CBHW080622290526

45790CB00007B/2886